To: Mark With thanks!

CW00816168

Architects
of a
Cleaner
Financial System

Thank you for your Work within Compliance.

TOLU' A. AKINYEMI

tolutoluo
11/09/2024

Cover Design: Buzz Designz

Published by 'The Roaring Lion Newcastle'

THE ROARING LION
NEWCASTLE

ISBN: 978-1-913636-44-9
eISBN: 978-1-913636-45-6

Email:
tolu@toluakinyemi.com
author@tolutoludo.com

Website:
www.toluakinyemi.com
www.tolutoludo.com

Preface

Being the first poet in recorded history to write a full-length poetry collection on financial crime compliance gives me tremendous joy.

I hope this collection of poems will be a useful addition to the bookshelf of leaders, devotees, enthusiasts, and students of financial crime compliance, and will become a reference point in years to come. These kinds of books help to deepen conversations from literary critics, industry players, and those who are looking to build a career within the industry. This could also be a way for newbies to gain an understanding of the terminologies within the industry without reading the policies and procedures of any single Financial Institution.

The idea for this book came out of a random conversation with my wife, when I informed her that I was interested in writing about this subject.

Fast-forward to a few days later, when I was ready to have a go and give this my best shot. As a writer who loves to think outside the box and challenge myself to do something extraordinary, I knew that if anyone could pull this off, I am the one who could make this happen.

This book is a testament that "your dreams are valid" and that whatever personal goals you have, the best time to start working toward them is now. And I hope you enjoy reading this collection of poems, which is my gift to the world. I consider it one of my significant works, given the subjects covered and the impact this is bound to have within the financial services sector.

Don't stop roaring!

Dedication

To everyone working assiduously day
and night to ensure we have safer
financial systems and institutions.

Acknowledgements

I'm grateful to God almighty for the gift of life, as life and being in good health is the premise that dreams and aspirations draw strength from.

Special thanks to my booktiful partner and friend, Olabisi, for the unending support on my literary journey. And to my charmazing children, Isaac and Abigail Akinyemi – thanks for your support and for always believing that the **great** 'Lion of Newcastle' is the best poet alive.

To my poetry editor, Julia Webb – thank you for the duty of care while editing this collection and the invaluable feedback.

Thank you to Diane Donovan for a final proofread of this collection.

Sincere appreciation to Nisha Joseph for being an early reader of this body of work, and for your insightful feedback.

To everyone who has supported me on my journey to literary acclaim – your support is greatly appreciated.

Contents

Know Your Customer

Your mother's maiden name
lives rent-free in your head,
but the lines on your palm
do not connect.

Would you
             identify and verify?
             Beam your searchlight into the
dark alleys?

Identify each soldier ant
from the multitude besieging the anthill.
Assess each red light with eagle eyes.
These risk factors cannot be bypassed.

Know your customer.
Know your customer.
Know your customer.

Know Your Customer (KYC)
*'Know Your Customer' are guidelines and regulations in
financial services that require professionals to verify the
identity, suitability, and risks involved in maintaining a
business relationship with a customer.*

Architects of a Cleaner Financial System

The first line of defence is gathering facts,
plugging gaps,
identifying and verifying related parties,
hunting for negative news, sniffing out errors.
A reputable coach
desperate for completeness and accuracy.
A four-eye checker cannot let it slide under the radar.

The second line of defence:
marksmen with precision.
The rules are blocking loopholes;
automated tools are speaking in familiar dialects.
Compliance programs are unwavering to these relentless attacks.

The third line of defence holds mounted roadblocks,
Audited on every trail. This independent assurance sweeps tides of risk.

The three lines of defence (or 3LOD) model is an accepted regulated framework designed to facilitate an effective risk management system.

The Four Eyes Principle is a widely used internal control mechanism that requires two individuals to review any activity that involves material risk profiles.

Curriculum Vitae

Fifteen years' experience
but there are weeds
growing
        across
             the
                     pond's surface.

How do we swim safely to harbour
With so many strings attached?

The job market is built
on a foundation of falsehood.
We are building blocks of exaggerated lies
that then fall apart like broken bricks.

Screening

Input your search strings with laser focus.
We are unearthing earth and mud.
Excavate down to the inner layers.
Separate debris from precious ornaments.

We are on a search mission for negative news.
Sanctions, these weighty barriers,
and politically exposed persons, are perennial
albatrosses. The hits are flying missiles.

Why would you discount this as a false
positive, without a rationale as thick as brick?
Locate the true hits that have made this home
a den for hideous characters.

*Adverse media screening is the process according to
which a customer, or prospective customer, is compared
to ("screened against") negative news and data
sources.*

*A politically exposed person (PEP) is an individual who
is or has been entrusted with a prominent function.
Many PEPs hold positions that can be abused for the
purpose of laundering illicit funds or other predicate
offences such as corruption or bribery.*

Holes

You have plastered over the gaping holes
that could raise a red flag.
The origin of these funds is mysterious,
and your explanation rooted in deceit.

Come to this compliance table cleaner
than sparkling water.
We are tilling the soil
for suspicious activity.

I'm on the trail of your every move,
hunting for red flags and
suspicious transactions. Why are these
transactions shrouded in secrecy?

*AML red flags are common warning signs alerting firms
and law enforcement to a suspicious transaction that
may involve money laundering.*

Placement

Illicit funds look for safe shelters
to disguise origins of tainted wealth
with instruments that cripple

and ripple through the financial system.
Illicit funds are on the hunt for cracks,
breaking windows and leaking roofs.

Illicit funds are crawling through the night,
hiding under the cover of darkness,
looking for a resting place.

*The placement stage in money laundering refers to the
initial introduction of "dirty" cash or illegal proceeds into
the financial system.*

Ultimate Beneficial Owner

The ownership chain is a long winding road
a tangled rope.
We have peeled the layers
and the revelations are an eyesore.

A mist of confusion
links these
placeholders
to the key holder.

We are drilling down into the ultimate links,
drilling
until we reveal
the Book of Revelations.

*An Ultimate Beneficial Owner is the person or entity who
is the ultimate beneficiary of the company.*

*The Financial Action Task Force (FATF) provides the
definition of the 'Ultimate Beneficial Owner' as: "the
natural person(s) who ultimately owns or controls a
customer and/or the natural person on whose behalf a
transaction is being conducted."*

Risk Appetite

My appetite for risk
is below sea level.
Simplify your due diligence.

A little chunk here
another bite of the cherry there
is my immunity from the hail and storms.

I have been stung by the bees of impropriety.
My appetite for risk hits imaginary roofs
and catapults into sinking sands.

Risk appetite is the level of risk that an organization is prepared to accept in pursuit of its objectives before action is deemed necessary to reduce the risk.

Slave of the Tax Master

I have been taxed to the bones
but the policymakers have their wealth
hidden in offshore tax havens.

My state pension age is a hill
to climb.

National insurance contributions
leave no assurance
of bliss
or happy endings.

I am imprisoned in this bracket of higher
taxes. I have sacrificed my salary
on the altar of a better future.

Offshore tax havens are frequently small, autonomous nations or territories that are situated in areas with a favourable tax climate. Switzerland, Bermuda, the British Virgin Islands, and the Cayman Islands are a few of the most well-known offshore tax havens.

National Insurance is a fundamental component of the welfare state in the United Kingdom. It acts as a form of social security, since the payment of NI contributions establishes entitlement to certain state benefits for workers and their families.

Experience

Wanted: an experienced hand.

Person of Special Interest
missing for ten years
and there is an army of bright stars
adorning the night sky.

Wanted: 24 karat pure gold
refined to immaculate standards
when there are multitudes of gold fishes
swimming through your mailbox.

Head Hunting: the perfect candidate
a replica of the replica
of the replica
who left through the fire exit.

You're looking for the wind
swirling through a revolving door
when you have unrefined gold
that needs polishing, swarming around you.

But, you have been blinded by your blind
quest.

High Risk

After Nigeria was added to Financial Action Task Force Grey List on February 24, 2023.

I am Nigerian, so High Risk.
Can't you see the labels shining? Haven't you heard we are home to notorious PEPs?

I am Nigerian, and am on FATF's Grey List.
Our deficiencies in countering money laundering, terrorist financing,

and proliferation financing is an entrenched cancer. I am Nigerian, and my only crime is a green passport and a blighted reputation.

The FATF grey list refers to the FATF's practice of publicly identifying countries with strategic Anti-Money Laundering and Countering the Financing of Terrorism (AML/CFT) deficiencies.

The purpose of implementing anti-money laundering and counter-terrorist financing (AML/CFT) measures is to stop criminals and terrorists from abusing the financial system.

Risk Mitigation

Mitigate the risk, lest we become casualties
of this consuming fire.

These spreading risks cannot be
watered down.

Mitigate the risk, lest our reputations
become shredded rags.

These bulging gaps cannot be
plugged by weak plausibility.

Mitigate the risk, lest the regulatory fines
leave us in the red,

trapped in the web
of swirling litigations.

Risk mitigation is about implementing controls to limit
the potential money laundering and terrorist financing
risks you have identified while conducting your risk
assessment to stay within your risk tolerance level.

Sanctions

We have blown hot air,
but it becomes a messy irritant.
Our blows to the jaw have missed their targets.

This grand finale is a shouting match.
We sanction and sanction
but are greeted with brutal reactions.

Egg me on
on this road to perdition.
Lead me to my crucible.

The ropes have been tightened again,
for the umpteenth time, but the whole scene
has the look of a comedy show.

Sanctions are restrictive measures imposed on individuals or entities with the aim to curtail their activities and to exert pressure and influence on them.

Fact-Finding

Oil magnate with no oil wells,
would you tell me the nature of your business?
Would you tell me how you amassed wealth
larger than water bodies?

The numbers are fighting silent wars.
Would you tell me about your little
beginnings? These rationales are moonlight
stories. Would you lay the facts bare

so I can unravel these mysteries?

We Are Showing Off Our Compliance Programs

Fireballs, tested instruments of war.
The hackers are mudslinging
and we are coming to this battlefield

with firewalls of resistance. Our artillery of
communications strikes-through
~~business email compromise scams.~~

The carnage boggles the mind.
Our compliance programs are standing up
to the filth and dirt blighting years of progress.

A compliance program is a set of internal policies and procedures within a company to comply with laws, rules, and regulations; or to uphold the business's reputation.

Business email compromise (or BEC) is a form of phishing attack where a criminal attempts to trick a senior executive (or budget holder) into transferring funds or revealing sensitive information.

Phishing

I am on a fishing expedition,
caught in a dragnet of hyperlinks;
flying with the precision of supersonic jets.

Your phishing ammunition is a weakling.
Report weak links in your fishing nets before
you become a casualty of your own greed.

Phishing is when attackers attempt to trick users into doing 'the wrong thing', such as clicking a bad link that will download malware or directing them to a questionable website.

PEPs as a Metaphor for State Capture

The state is in chains of politically exposed
persons. Instruments of state are comatose
and the wings of honourable men have been
clipped. Corruption sails at high altitudes

and men of devious means
sit on the exalted seats of government.
The police are a force of brutality and our
justices have dipped their hands in the mud.

The gods have been soiled.
The gods have defied sacred places.
The gods of the masses are
shrunken shrubs.

Financial Crime Fighter

Your LinkedIn headline screams perfection
but you're a disjointed wheel.

Red flags have been raised time and again
and suspicious activities have devoured fine
woods, but you are blind to the signs.

The field is larger than the Santiago Bernabeu,
but there is no room to disappear into obscure
places. Here, you carry the burden of sanctity
and sanitising against looming warfare.

The consequences of laxity could be a date
on a stake, or burning to ashes
those fanciful LinkedIn titles.

Deterrent

I have so many poetic lines
and verses
that would leave your heart
tangled with mine.

But, the dusty ring on my shelf
is a deal-breaker.
I have so many memorable hymns,
my heart rends for you

But, my conjugal status is a deterrent
that kills the flame of our fledgling love.
I have so many secrets to leak
to you-

but the fear of regulatory fines and sanctions
have kept me wedged to the stake of equity

forever.

Regulatory Fines means any civil monetary fine or penalty imposed by a federal, state, local, or foreign governmental entity in such entity's regulatory or official capacity, pursuant to its order under a Regulatory Proceeding.

Risk Appetite Statement

My appetite for risk is at an all-time low
and I treat every penny and pound
as a treasure of value.
I am a bundle of risk

and life is a melting pot of uncertainty
that sends my emotions into overdrive.
Through the darkness of night
there is a risk of slipping into the unknown.

My risk appetite statement is a contrived mess.
How do I tick the boxes that matter?
Risk of falling, failing,
or a million and one ways to take the plunge.

The risk of having no appetite to navigate
dark patches that might blemish our paths
erase the appetite to bear the burdens of these
forces.

A Risk Appetite Statement is a statement of the level and type of risk the organization is willing to take to meet its objectives.

Cash Intensive

Your card machine is stalling
installing updates: a slow train.
It's another piece of furniture in this shop
that flows with cold cash.

The tricks in your playbook have been blown
open wide, and the sweet fragrance of tax
evasion consumes the atmosphere.

You say "nothing to declare."
The hens have hatched in the market square
and the orchestra of contortionists
has exposed hidden secrets.

We are hiding behind veils and
clandestine instruments. These fronts
are affronts to our collective interests.

*Tax evasion is an illegal attempt to defeat the imposition
of taxes by individuals, corporations, trusts, and others.*

Dirty Money

Dirty money is a flowing river.
It crosses borders before commingling,
undetected, with clean money.

Dirty money is flying in all directions
to secret locations and
tax havens.

Dirty money is causing a firestorm:
it charred the oak tree
until it became a ghost.

Dirty money is fighting unseen wars,
and we are battle-weary
from this conflagration,

signposted

with burning smoke.

Money obtained from certain crimes, such as extortion, insider trading, drug trafficking, and illegal gambling, is "dirty" and needs to be "cleaned" to appear to have been derived from legal activities, so that banks and other financial institutions will deal with it without suspicion.

Know Your Bank

I want to know my bank
like I know my partner;
unravel the secrets hidden
from the regulators' radar.

I want to know how my bank
tracks my every move;
sends me endless notifications
that leave me feeling vulnerable.

I want to know the real bank
beyond the public spectacle;
the semblance
of a grand coverup.

Bonds

My bonds give me immense joy.
They wear the garment of my words:
Low Risk
true to type.

When the stocks and shares experience
is an upheaval
rocking solid ground,

my bonds are chords
striking hope.
The riffs douse a tension
that rises like boiling water.

Bonds are issued by governments and corporations when they want to raise money. By buying a bond, you're giving the issuer a loan, and they agree to pay you back the face value of the loan on a specific date, and to pay you periodic interest payments along the way-usually twice a year.

Risk Assessments

I

This relationship is at a boiling point
and the divorce papers await signatures.
The purpose of relationship is at odds with
your words, which were once coated with

honey. The car has veered off its course.
Ominous clouds gather.
We are assessing the risks
that are a signal of what's to come.

II

I'm assessing this relationship again.
This is toxic;
a loaded gun.
The air is melancholic

and sorrowful music paints a dark picture.
I have been blinded
by familiar spirits and tokenism -
enticing roadblocks

for potential client exits.

An AML risk assessment helps identify the institution's
inherent risk and assesses the effectiveness of its
preventative and detective controls.

We Have Upped the Ante
Against Financial Crime

Setting immaculate standards,
our policies and procedures
are worthy combatants,

shooting down any weaknesses
that could pose a risk.
We have discarded ruinous paths.

When the door was left ajar,
the free-for-all carnage
and regulatory fines dealt us crushing blows.

Customer Onboarding

We are aboard a ship
navigating stormy seas
but the dynamics are ever-changing.

We are monitoring
for changing weather
and sea pirates who want to

attack
attack
attack

Open your eyes to the controls,
an artillery of disruption to the
status quo.

II

Beware of strange bedfellows.
This onboarding subject is not as easy as ABC.
Assess the purpose of relationships
and exterminate the risks before they

terminate us.
The financial institutions that allowed rainfalls
of improprieties were washed away
by the fiery storms.

This marriage proposal would require
enhanced due diligence, not standard or
simplified. We won't onboard with
incomplete documentation.

Identify,
verify, evaluate all risks
before you join us together and pronounce
those delicate words: 'till death do us part.'

*The KYC onboarding process refers to the steps a
business must take in order to verify a customer's true
identity and risk level.*

Enhanced Due Diligence (EDD) is the highest level of
due diligence that can then be performed as part of a
Risk-Based Approach.

Risky Border

This border leaks drugs
in gargantuan proportions.

A porous sieve.

This border is a laundromat
washing dirty laundry.

Drug peddlers are emboldened lions.

This risky border is a terminal point
where dreams are staked

and laid to rest.

A Laundromat is an all-purpose financial vehicle, typically set up by a bank or other financial services company, that is intended to help clients launder the proceeds of crime, hide ownership of assets, embezzle funds from companies, evade taxes or currency restrictions, and move money offshore.

Dreaded Regulatory Fines

The news screamers have landed body blows
and our reputations have been ripped
into shredded pieces.

Poisoned chalices
dodge the bullets.
The morning after is a sordid mess.

There is a fine line,
threaded, between regulatory fines:
sour limes of discomfort.

Our Love Was Event Driven

Let's review.
Her soft-spoken words
melted my heart like wax.

Here are the triggers.
There was a merger of two hearts:
a conduit pipe of love's attraction.

We have been to the Eiffel Tower,
padlocked our hearts, and thrown the key
into the river.

Our love was an event-driven soap opera, and
high risk.

Virtual Currency

Unregulated currencies are pots of risk.
Alternative reality,
furious birds crying in the open space.
Digital tears cannot be wiped

with manual commiserations.
My appetite for risky ventures is
on the floor
blemished by bees of irregularities.

That stung,
and the cost-of-living crisis
holds me captive
in the throes of unmitigated poverty.

*A virtual currency is a type of digital currency that only
exists in electronic form and includes many types of
currencies, including cryptocurrency.*

Code of Conduct

Sing a dirge for conduct rules.
Write an elegy for the reign of absurdity.

The entrenched rules of engagement
are forgotten songs.

Write a sad poem for conflict of interest:
many interests are on a collision course.

We are falling for the bait of
temporary gratification

filling our pockets
with sour lemons and dirty oil.

A code of conduct is a set of rules outlining the norms, rules, and responsibilities or proper practices of an individual party or an organization.

Correspondent Banking

The customers of my customers are unknown species. Combustible elements crisscross our channels. The money trail is disguising its clandestine mission.

Customer identification programs stand on feeble ground. This bromance with high-risk jurisdictions, paper banks, and respondent banks are an encumbrance

that might stain our stainless records.

Correspondent banking is the provision of banking services by one bank (the "correspondent bank") to another bank (the "respondent bank"). Large international banks typically act as correspondents for thousands of other banks around the world.

The Customer Identification Program sets the minimum requirements for onboarding new clients, but depending on the size and location of an organization, each program will vary.

High-risk jurisdictions have significant strategic deficiencies in their regimes to counter money laundering, terrorist financing, and the financing of proliferation.

Risk-Based Approach

This review has not been engraved in the sand.
Can you spot the patterns?
Assess the risks mounting
as roadblocks.

We are not following a one-way road.
The risks drive the approach. Town roads are
different from motorways. This blanket
approach is a metaphor for disaster.

A risk-based approach means that countries, competent authorities, and banks identify, assess, and understand the money laundering and terrorist financing risk to which they are exposed, and take the appropriate mitigation measures in accordance with the level of risk.

Identity Theft

My password is for sale on the dark web.
I'm a vulnerable mouse
amid hungry cats.

Dark Web activity detected.
Norton's notification makes me blue
Twitter (200m) accounts

My email, username,
and full name
are in the cat's mouth.

Identity theft is when your personal details are stolen,
and identity fraud is when those details are used to
commit fraud.

Twitter (200m) accounts: Hackers stole the email
addresses of over 200 million Twitter users and posted
them on an online hacking forum.

Account Blocks

I went to the altar this morning;
made a vow to uphold the tenets of
treating customers fairly.

I arrive at work this morning
and I have an account blocks list.
I'm lost in a web of guilty entanglements.

How do I cut off the pipeline of funds
from a dying husband in intensive care?

How do I stop food supplies to a family
whose stomachs will groan tonight?

How do I wear thick layers when the aftermath
reverberates louder than an earthquake?

These customers aren't fair game.

I went to bed tonight knowing I treated
customers fairly, and I'm free from the web of
guilt.

A blocked account generally refers to a
financial account that has some limitations or
restrictions placed upon it, temporarily or permanently.

Fraud Checks

The technique is
a mountain of deceit
that fleeces the innocent
leeches

The dream is:
to decrease the naive
broken
pieces

leeches
fleeces
with eloquent speeches,
and heartaches increases.

Screening Tools

Lexis Nexis is dung.
Its stench cannot be described with flowery
words. Dow Jones (PEPs & Sanctions
Screening) has unmasked your true identity.

These smokescreens are a shattered glass.
We have just screened on Factiva
and the facts hurt the imagination.

World Check checks the word
exposing hidden sanctions and
PEP links.
Checkmate.

Alacra
Alacra
Alacra

We are
screening
screening
screening

until we remove the smokescreens
of negative news
and undetected crime
that loom like an albatross.

LexisNexis helps uncover the information that commercial organizations, government agencies, and non-profits need to get a complete picture of individuals, businesses, and assets with industry-leading data and analytic solutions.

Dow Jones Risk & Compliance offers politically exposed persons (PEPs) and sanctions screening solutions for firms of all sizes.

Factiva is an archive of over 32,000 major global newspapers, newswires, industry publications, magazines, reports, and other sources.

World-Check is a database of structured profiles on people and entities known to represent a direct reputation, financial, or compliance risk.

The River of Exploitation Overflows With Pain

Vicious activities are circling eagles
and the vulnerable are victims.
Elderly abuse is an intruding gale.
Trust is in deficit;
trusted persons are parasites, preying.

The vulnerable are resisting vicious attacks,
flooding spam in
a wide array of scams.

Strangers are firing shots,
testing the armoury.
Malware is shooting down life savings,
phonies, clones, and even the state.

Don't fall into the cesspit of lethal love.
The sweepstakes have swept many to the
stake.
Sniff out the patterns:
emergencies from loved ones are a red flag.
See the red light.
STOP!
VERIFY!!!

*Malware is a catch-all term for any type of malicious
software designed to harm or exploit any programmable
device, service, or network. Cybercriminals typically use
it to extract data that they can leverage over victims for
financial gain.*

Know Your Customer II

We are removing the masks
that obscure identities.
Stand in line
for your verification checks.

We are travelling into the past.
The source of wealth assessments
cannot be waived away.
We are monitoring transactions,

Sieving for the unusual.
Mysterious sources of funds cannot
escape such intense scrutiny. Our appetite
for odd behaviour is below sea level.

Can you spot the trends—
unfamiliar patterns
flowing through?
Follow the trail.

*Source of wealth relates to activities that generated or
contributed to the client's overall net worth or wealth
and how they came to possess the funds for the
transaction – i.e. investments or a company sale.*

Entities

Unknown entities are disrupting
the status quo.
The Special Purpose Vehicle has broken down-
a dysfunctional tool past its sell-by date.

I no longer hedge against risky funds.
I'm running away from
naked trusts. In God I trust.
Every other trust is quicksand.

Charities lay foundations - weak
break the yoke,
crack eggs of risky enterprises,
avoid this splattered mess

across boards
and entities conveying
momentous risks
that hit harder than a tremor.

*A special purpose vehicle, also called a special purpose
entity (SPE), is a subsidiary created by a parent
company to isolate financial risk.*

*Naked trusts are trusts in which the trustee has no duty
other than to transfer the property to the beneficiary.*

Insider Trading

This is a love letter to my bank.
The pen spills ink
and the heart weaves solemn words.

The roots of distrust have grown into
clusters of overgrown weeds
and I am the victim.

When insider trading hit like a brutal quake
and the executives feasted
on my blood and sweat

that was the breaking point.

*Insider trading is buying or selling a publicly traded
company's stock by someone with non-public, material
information about that company.*

Interest Rates

After the Bank of England increased interest rates for the eleventh consecutive time by 0.25% to 4.25% on the 23rd of March, 2023.

The Bank of England
duels with inflation.
Firecrackers, we are the remnants
of the fireworks.

The interest rate is a rising spring
inflation is causing an uprising
the interest rate has grown thorns
and we are greenhorns to this buffeting storm.

The interest rate is on the rise
inflation has swallowed sweet cravings,
beaten the brave,
flattened fat wallets.

The Bank of England wrestles inflation
and the casualties of these body blows
are washed like sand onto the
seashore.

The Bank of England (BoE) is the UK's central bank.

The rate of inflation is the change in prices for goods and services over time. Measures of inflation and prices include consumer price inflation, producer price inflation, and the House Price Index.

Interest is what you pay for borrowing money, and what banks pay you for saving money with them. Interest rates are shown as a percentage of the amount you borrow or save over a year.

Camouflage

Cleaning money
washing money
laundering money
recycling money

this is an integration game.

Buy a yacht
a cash-starved football club
a moribund business.

Identify soft targets
and weak castles;
circle the orbit.

Investment vehicles are in full motion

Wash dirty money
in an endless cycle
before our grand re-entrance,
whiter than snowfall.

Integration is the final stage of a money laundering process where the money is reintroduced to the legal economy. In integration, the money is re-introduced into the legal economy after a series of reconditioning moves. This is done to give the money a legitimate appearance.

I'm Having Trust Issues
With My Bank

Two banks dead. Unknown numbers are
walking corpses. The last financial crisis

was an endless passageway.
I won't write a dirge for a dying bank.

Two banks on the precipice
and buzzing alarms shadow it all.

Two banks are vanishing clouds
and the frenzied waves rattle like thunder.

Two banks tip off the edge
and we are teetering on the verge

of another looming financial crisis.

AB & C, AML, AFC, ETC....

Anti-bribery
and corruption are

not selective choices.
I am not running agendas
or selling false narratives.

Anti-Money Laundering
Anti-Financial Crime

Frisk me
to my bare bottom.
My hands are spotless.

Anti-terrorism
Anti-Fraud

We are not suited to your holy wars
or terrorist inclinations.
Frauds
brainwashed children of perdition.

Angling for burning fame and
clutching the wind,
we have upped the ante
and our anti-wars are in full motion.

Pyrrhic Victory

We are sourcing congratulatory messages
for my tribesman,
the new president-select.
A pyrrhic victory tastes of sour,
sour lemons.

The ruling party is restless in their
jaundiced victory,
barking like hypnotised dogs.
these tracks are a burgeoning minefield

Propaganda is matching propaganda,
the kite of misinformation is airborne,
and fake news
pillage sane minds.

Don't stand for the truth.
The label would be: bastard child.
I won't write a letter to America;
elections there are not spotless garments.

A sage says, *don't throw mud*.
at our President-Select:
he could be the best yet.
I won't throw a tea party

for electoral fraudsters,
impostors,
and gaslighters
who stand truth on its head.

Partnership

My sleeping partner
wants the spoils of war.
I won't raise my middle finger
or scream blue murder.

No offence—
I am a crusader for women's rights; a
bastion of equality
behind closed doors and in full glare.

I have had a few friends, poets,
who are equalist for perception.
Eat the serpent's apple, or two—
a worthy price to pay.

Gay boy for show.
Western media friendly.
I won't trade a vagina or two
to become a portrait.

Cut for perception
to suit narrations
that never pop you into the limelight
beyond labels and fleeting appraisals.

A partnership is a type of business structure in which two or more parties share ownership of the business.

Bearer Shares

Hide the ownership;
remove our secrets from full view.
Stand in the gap.
The full picture will cause heads to roll.

This is a bearer's game—
bearer of good news
bearer of bad news
and I am the bearer only in name.

*Bearer shares are unregistered securities whose owners
have a physical share certificate with them.*

Money-Making Machine

Analog poet, old money man,
I have not invested
a penny in bitcoin
or crypto.

I'm no longer desperate
to double my wealth.
Money-making machines are wild illusions.
I am a realist.

I no longer dream about heavenly
Manna.
The perpetual direct debits
deserve all the credit.

Perhaps I should write a book
on how not to become prey
to money wolves,
and sugary scams.

Bitcoin (BTC) is a cryptocurrency, a virtual currency designed to act as money and a form of payment outside the control of any one person, group, or entity, thus removing the need for third-party involvement in financial transactions.

Hunted

The wild is swirling in turmoil
and the extermination cymbal beats,
distorted by nature.

The forests burn
at every turn
and climate wears a chameleon's skin.
Habitats have been swallowed up by

storming floods.
Human exploitation regurgitates
and all species are at risk of   looming
~~extinction.~~

A Poet's Rant

I am not without sin,
hauling my bulky
baggage
from exes and failed partnerships.

Spot the signs.
Society is riddled with filthy money;
gales of ruin.

We are on the trail of money mules,
paint mules with brushes of criminality.
Easy money comes with gripes
and throat grime.

I am a writer at risk.
This burden of truth
is a howling wind.
Fraud and crime are resisting waves.

I am fighting for my life
with word spears and poetic shields
protecting me from the barrage of enemy
attacks.

*A money mule is someone who lets someone else use
their bank account to transfer money, often keeping a
little bit for themselves.*

Fleeting

Hush has been hushed
into the silent night
and Woodberry
has tasted sour berries.

The glitz and blitz
have been tainted by foul air
and the army of soldier ants
no longer besiege their honeypot.

Tell the sons in the hinterland
that these paths have been watermarked
by calamity.

These paths reek of perdition
and a hushed life
behind wooden bars.

Ramon Olorunwa Abbas, commonly known as Hushpuppi, Hush or Ray Hushpuppi, is a Nigerian former Instagram influencer and convicted felon.

Olalekan Ponle, better known as Woodberry, is an ally of Ramon Abbas, best known as Hushpuppi, another Nigerian international fraudster, who was jailed in November 2022.

Compliance Poet

My resume reads: Compliance Poet –
Certified Anti-Money Laundering Specialist;
author of a collection of financial crime
compliance poems
and over twenty books.

Let the stars align.
Let the heavens pour rain and
show a rainbow of acceptance.

The regulations are swimming in my head.
I'm plotting graphs
analysing entry points.

Sanctions advisory, AML advisory,
compliance roles,
risks and controls—the list is endless.

There are no embargoes to aspirations,
no restrictions or sanctions,
no limitation on ambition.

Dare to fly on the wings of dreams.
Maybe, just maybe, your career pathway
will align like the stars.

Author's Note

Thank you for the time you have taken to read this book. I hope you enjoyed the poems in it.

If you loved the book and have a minute to spare, I would appreciate a short review on the page or site where you bought it. I greatly appreciate your help in promoting my work. Reviews from readers like you make a huge difference in helping new readers choose a book.

Thank you!
Tolu' A. Akinyemi

Author's Bio

Tolu' A. Akinyemi (also known as Tolutoludo and the Lion of Newcastle) is a multiple award-winning author in the genres of poetry, short stories, children's literature, and essays. His works include Dead Lions Don't Roar (poetry, 2017); Unravel Your Hidden Gems (essays, 2018); Dead Dogs Don't Bark (poetry, 2018); Dead Cats Don't Meow (poetry, 2019); Never Play Games With the Devil (poetry, 2019); Inferno of Silence (short stories, 2020); A Booktiful Love (poetry, 2020); Black ≠ Inferior (poetry, 2021); Never Marry a Writer (poetry, 2021); Everybody Don Kolomental (poetry, 2021); I Wear Self-Confidence Like a Second Skin (children's literature, 2021); I Am Not a Troublemaker (children's literature, 2021); Born in Lockdown (poetry, 2021); A God in a Human Body (poetry, 2022); If You Have To Be Anything, Be Kind (children's literature, 2022); City of Lost Memories, (poetry, 2022); Awaken Your Inner Lion, (essays, 2022); On The Train To Hell, (poetry, 2022); You Need More Than Dreams (poetry, 2023); and The Morning Cloud is Empty (poetry, 2023).

A former headline act at Great Northern Slam, Havering Literary Festival, Crossing The Tyne Festival, and Feltonbury Arts and Music Festival, he also inspires large audiences through spoken word performances and has appeared as a keynote speaker in major forums and events. He facilitates creative writing master classes for many audiences.

His poems have appeared (or are forthcoming) in the 57th issue (Volume 15, No. 1) of the Wilderness House Literary Review; The Writers Cafe Magazine (Issue 18); GN Books; Lion and Lilac; Agape Review; Continue the Voice; My Woven Poetry; Black Moon Magazine; Calla Press; African Writer Magazine; The Football in Poetry 2nd Anthology; and elsewhere.

His poems have been translated into Greek.

His books are based on a deep reality and often reflect relationships and life, featuring people he has met in his journey as a writer. His books have inspired many people to improve their performances and/or their circumstances. Tolu' has taken his poetry to the stage, performing his written words at many events. Through his writing and these performances, he supports business leaders, other aspiring authors, and people of all ages who are interested in reading and writing. Sales of the books have allowed Tolu' donate to charity, allowing him to make a difference where he feels it's important and showing that he lives by the words he puts to page.

He is a co-founder of Lion and Lilac, a UK-based arts organisation, and sits on the board of many organisations.

Tolu' is a financial crime consultant as well as a Certified Anti-Money Laundering Specialist (CAMS) with extensive experience working with leading investment banks and consultancy firms.

He is a trained economist from Ekiti State University (formerly known as University of Ado-Ekiti (UNAD)).

He sat for his master's degree in Accounting and Financial Management at the University of Hertfordshire, Hatfield, United Kingdom.

Tolu' was a student ambassador at the University of Hertfordshire, Hatfield, representing the university in major forums and engaging with young people during various assignments.

Tolu' Akinyemi was born in Ado-Ekiti, Nigeria and lives in the United Kingdom. Tolu' is an ardent supporter of Chelsea Football Club in London.

You can connect with Tolu' on his various social media accounts:

Instagram: @ToluToludo
Facebook: facebook.com/toluaakinyemi
Twitter: @ToluAkinyemi | @ToluToludo

Dead Lions Don't Roar

In a society where moral rectitude is increasingly becoming abeyant, Akinyemi's bounden duty is to reawaken it with verses. He, thus, functions as a philosopher-poet, a kind of factotum inculcating wisdom in different facets of life. Dead Lions Don't Roar leads us into the universe of an exact mind rousing the lethargic from indolence or prevarication, bearing in mind that the greatest achievers are those who take the bull by the horn. Taking a step can just be the open sesame to reach the stars. Enough of jeremiad! - **The Sun**

Dead Lions Don't Roar, a collection of poetic wisdom for the discerning, makes an interesting read. A paper pack, the poems are concise, easy to digest, travel friendly and express deep feelings and noble thoughts in beautiful and simple language. **-The Nation**

Akinyemi's verses are concise, straight-edge and explanatory, reminiscent of the kind of poetry often churned out by Mamman J. Vatsa, the late soldier and poet. **–yNaija**

Dead Lion's Don't Roar is a collection of inspiring and motivating modern-day verses. Addressing many issues close to home and also many taboo subjects, the poetry is reflective of today's struggles, and lights the way to a positive future. The uplifting book will appeal to all age groups and anyone going through change, building or enjoying a career, and facing day to day struggles. Many of the short verses will resonate with readers, leaving a sense of peace and wellbeing.

Inferno of Silence

Poignant and honest...
Akinyemi's first collection of short stories dazzles with elegant prose, genuine emotions, and Nigerian cultural lore as it plumbs both the socio-cultural issues and the depths of love, loss, grief, and personal trauma. Lovers of literary fiction will be rewarded. - **The Prairies Book Review**

The first collection of short stories by this multitalented author entwines everyday events that are articulated in excellent storytelling.

The title story "Inferno of Silence" portrays men's societal challenges and the unspoken truths and burdens that men bear, while "Black lives Matter" shows the firsthand trauma of a man facing racism as a footballer plying his trade in Europe.

Stories range from "Return Journey" where we encounter a techpreneur/ Poet/Serial Womanizer confronting consequences of his past actions, to "Blinded by Silence," where a couple united by love must face a political upheaval changing their fortune.

These are completed with stories of relationships: "Trouble in Umudike" – about family wealth and marriage; "Everybody don Kolomental" where the main character deals with mental health issues; and "In the Trap of Seers" when one's life is on auto-reverse with the death of her confidante, her mother, as she takes us through her ordeal and journey to redemption. This is a broad and very inclusive collection.

BLACK ≠INFERIOR

Poetry readers interested in the fusion of literary ability and social inspection will appreciate the hard-hitting blend of both in *Black#Inferior,* which is recommended reading for a wide audience, especially students of Black experience.- *D. Donovan - Senior Reviewer, Midwest Book Review.*

A celebration of black culture and experience and life in general, the collection makes for an electrifying read. - *The Prairies Book Review.*

Black ≠ Inferior is a collection of poems divided into 2 parts. The first part is a collection of thematically linked poems exploring Blackness and the myriads of issues it attracts. The second part oscillates themes— talking about consent, a query of death, a celebration of love among others. In his usual stylistic, this collection deals with weighty matters like race and colourism with simple and clear language.

In Black ≠ Inferior, we see Tolu' Akinyemi reacting in response to the world, to issues that affect Black people. Here, we see a poet shedding off his burdens through his poems; hence, the beauty of this collection is in the issues it attempts to address. In this collection, Tolu' wears a coat of many colours – he is a preacher, a prophet, a doctor and a teacher.

We see Tolu' the preacher in these lines:
'I wish you can rise through the squalor of poverty and voices that watercolour you as under-represented. I wish you can emblaze your name in gold, and swim against every wave of hate.'

This is a collection of poems fit for the present narrative as any (Black) person who reads this collection should beam with confidence at the end. This is what the poet sets out to achieve with his oeuvre.

EVERYBODY DON KOLOMENTAL

A poignant collection that captures both the raw sorrows and joys of human existence.... --- "The Prairies Book Review"

Hope is Not Far Away...

Everybody Don Kolomental is a collection of poems that deal with everyday universal struggles.

Tolu' peddles hope to the lost and hopeless and pulls at the emotional strings of the heart in this collection of heartfelt poems. The collection mirrors life through the eyes of a deep-thinker and wordsmith.

Poet Tolu' A. Akinyemi knows the gravity of mental health struggles and uses his words as a soothing balm to heal readers of this collection.

In the poem titled 'Hope is not Far Away', he writes:

"Who will tell Okikiola that hope is not far away?

Its ship docked in the home of Akinyele before his candle was blown out and his flailing dreams were a shipwreck.

Who will tell Okikiola this is not the last straw?

These wind gusts would give way for the calming sea."

Whether you're in need of calm after the storm, therapy, healing, or to view everyday struggles from the lens of a veteran poet, this collection is for you.

71

Printed in Great Britain
by Amazon